FAVORITE BRAND NAME

Comfort Food

Publications International, Ltd.

Favorite Brand Name Recipes at www.fbnr.com

Microwave Cooking: Microwave ovens vary in wattage. Use the cooking times as guidelines and check for doneness before adding more time.

Preparation/Cooking Times: Preparation times are based on the approximate amount of time required to assemble the recipe before cooking, baking, chilling or serving. These times include preparation steps such as measuring, chopping and mixing. The fact that some preparations and cooking can be done simultaneously is taken into account. Preparation of optional ingredients and serving suggestions is not included.

table of contents

breakfast favorites

Oven-Baked French Toast

Makes 6 servings

12 slices cinnamon bread or cinnamon raisin bread
1 pint (16 ounces) half and half or light cream
2 large eggs
6 tablespoons I CAN'T BELIEVE IT'S NOT BUTTER!® Spread, melted
2 tablespoons firmly packed brown sugar
2 teaspoons vanilla extract
1 teaspoon grated orange peel (optional)
¼ teaspoon ground cinnamon
⅛ teaspoon ground nutmeg (optional)

Preheat oven to 350°F.

In lightly greased 13×9-inch baking pan, arrange bread slices in two layers.

In large bowl with wire whisk, blend remaining ingredients. Evenly pour over bread slices, pressing bread down until some liquid is absorbed and bread does not float. Bake 45 minutes or until center reaches 160°F. and bread is golden brown. Serve hot and sprinkle, if desired, with confectioners' sugar.

Cook's Tip: Freeze leftover French toast in airtight container. To reheat, let come to room temperature, then arrange on baking sheet and bake at 350°F. until hot.

Oven-Baked French Toast

Blueberry Orange Muffins

Makes 12 muffins

1¾ cups all-purpose flour
⅓ cup sugar
2½ teaspoons baking powder
½ teaspoon baking soda
½ teaspoon salt
½ teaspoon ground cinnamon
1 egg, slightly beaten
¾ cup fat-free (skim) milk
¼ cup butter, melted and slightly cooled
3 tablespoons orange juice concentrate, thawed
1 teaspoon vanilla
¾ cup fresh or frozen blueberries, thawed

1. Preheat oven to 400°F. Grease muffin pan or line with paper baking cups.

2. Combine flour, sugar, baking powder, baking soda, salt and cinnamon in large bowl. Set aside. Beat egg, milk, butter, orange juice concentrate and vanilla in medium bowl on medium speed of electric mixer until well combined. Add milk mixture to dry ingredients. Mix lightly until dry ingredients are barely moistened (mixture will be lumpy). Add blueberries. Stir gently just until berries are evenly distributed.

3. Fill muffin cups ¾ full. Bake 20 to 25 minutes (25 to 30 minutes if using frozen berries) or until toothpick inserted into centers comes out clean. Remove pan and allow to cool 5 minutes. Remove to wire rack. Serve warm.

Blueberry Orange Muffins

Southern Caramel Pecan Rolls

Makes 24 rolls

Topping

⅔ **cup sifted powdered sugar**

⅔ **cup dark brown sugar**

½ **cup whipping cream**

1 **teaspoon vanilla**

 PAM® No-Stick Cooking Spray

1 **cup coarsely chopped pecans**

Rolls

1 **cup dark raisins**

⅓ **cup brandy**

2 **(1-pound) loaves frozen sweet or white bread dough,**
 thawed, but not doubled in size

¼ **cup WESSON® Best Blend Oil**

½ **cup packed dark brown sugar**

1 **tablespoon ground cinnamon**

½ **teaspoon ground nutmeg**

TOPPING

In a medium bowl, stir together sugars, whipping cream and vanilla. Spray two 9×1½-inch round cake pans with PAM® Cooking Spray. Evenly divide mixture between pans and sprinkle with pecans; set aside pans.

ROLLS

In a small bowl, soak raisins in brandy for 30 minutes; set aside and stir occasionally.

On floured surface, roll *each* loaf into 12×8×¼-inch rectangle. Generously brush *each* sheet of dough with Wesson® Oil. In a small bowl, mix together brown sugar, cinnamon and nutmeg. Sprinkle over dough; top with soaked raisins. Roll up rectangles jelly-roll style starting with long edge. Pinch dough to seal. Cut into 12 slices. Place rolls, spiral side down, in cake pans. Cover with towels and let rise in warm place for 30 minutes or until nearly double in size. Preheat oven to 375°F. Bake, uncovered, for 15 to 20 minutes. Cover pans with foil to prevent overbrowning and bake an additional 10 minutes. Cool in pans 7 minutes. Invert onto serving plate. Best when served warm.

Southern Caramel Pecan Rolls

Streusel Coffeecake

Makes 24 servings

Prep Time: 25 minutes
Cook Time: 40 minutes
Cooling Time: 2 hours
Total Time: 3 hours and 5 minutes

> **32 CHIPS AHOY!® Chocolate Chip Cookies, divided**
> **1 (18- to 18.5-ounce) package yellow or white cake mix**
> **½ cup BREAKSTONE'S® or KNUDSEN® Sour Cream**
> **½ cup PLANTERS® Pecans, chopped**
> **½ cup BAKER'S® ANGEL FLAKE® Coconut**
> **¼ cup packed brown sugar**
> **1 teaspoon ground cinnamon**
> **⅓ cup margarine or butter, melted**
> **Powdered sugar glaze (optional)**

1. Coarsely chop 20 cookies; finely crush remaining 12 cookies. Set aside.

2. Prepare cake mix batter according to package directions; blend in sour cream. Stir in chopped cookies. Pour batter into greased and floured 13×9×2-inch baking pan.

3. Mix remaining cookie crumbs, pecans, coconut, brown sugar and cinnamon; stir in margarine or butter. Sprinkle over cake batter.

4. Bake at 350°F for 40 minutes or until toothpick inserted into center of cake comes out clean. Cool completely. Drizzle with powdered sugar glaze, if desired. Cut into squares to serve.

Streusel Coffeecake

Egg & Sausage Casserole
Makes 6 servings

½ **pound pork sausage**
3 **tablespoons margarine or butter, divided**
2 **tablespoons all-purpose flour**
¼ **teaspoon salt**
¼ **teaspoon black pepper**
1¼ **cups milk**
2 **cups frozen hash brown potatoes**
4 **eggs, hard-boiled and sliced**
½ **cup cornflake crumbs**
¼ **cup sliced green onions**

1. Preheat oven to 350°F. Spray 2-quart oval baking dish with nonstick cooking spray.

2. Crumble sausage into large skillet; brown over medium-high heat until no longer pink, stirring to separate meat. Drain sausage on paper towels. Discard fat and wipe skillet with paper towel.

3. Melt 2 tablespoons margarine in same skillet over medium heat. Stir in flour, salt and pepper until smooth. Gradually stir in milk; cook and stir until thickened. Add sausage, potatoes and eggs; stir to combine. Pour into prepared dish.

4. Melt remaining 1 tablespoon margarine. Combine cornflake crumbs and melted margarine in small bowl; sprinkle evenly over casserole.

5. Bake, uncovered, 30 minutes or until hot and bubbly. Sprinkle with onions.

Egg & Sausage Casserole

simmering soups

Potato Soup with Green Chilies & Cheese

Makes 6 servings

    2 tablespoons vegetable oil
    1 medium onion, chopped
    1 clove garlic, minced
    2 cups chopped unpeeled potatoes
    1 tablespoon all-purpose flour
 1½ cups chicken broth
    2 cups milk
    1 can (4 ounces) diced green chilies, undrained
    ½ teaspoon celery salt
    ¾ cup (3 ounces) shredded Monterey Jack cheese
    ¾ cup (3 ounces) shredded Colby or Cheddar cheese
       White pepper

Heat oil in 3-quart pan over medium heat. Add onion and garlic; cook until onion is tender. Stir in potatoes; cook 1 minute. Stir in flour; continue cooking 1 minute. Stir in broth. Bring to a boil. Cover; *reduce heat* and simmer 20 minutes or until potatoes are tender. Stir in milk, chilies and celery salt; heat to simmering. Add cheeses; stir and heat just until cheeses melt. Do not boil. Add pepper to taste. Serve in individual bowls. Garnish as desired.

Potato Soup with Green Chilies & Cheese

Hearty Chicken and Rice Soup

Makes 8 servings

> 10 cups chicken broth
> 1 medium onion, chopped
> 1 cup sliced celery
> 1 cup sliced carrots
> ¼ cup snipped fresh parsley
> ½ teaspoon cracked black pepper
> ½ teaspoon dried thyme leaves
> 1 bay leaf
> 1½ cups cubed chicken (about ¾ pound)
> 2 cups cooked rice
> 2 tablespoons lime juice
> Lime slices for garnish

Combine broth, onion, celery, carrots, parsley, pepper, thyme and bay leaf in Dutch oven. Bring to a boil; stir once or twice. Reduce heat; simmer, uncovered, 10 to 15 minutes. Add chicken; simmer, uncovered, 5 to 10 minutes or until chicken is no longer pink in center. Remove and discard bay leaf. Stir in rice and lime juice just before serving. Garnish with lime slices.

Favorite recipe from *USA Rice Federation*

Rapid Ragú® Chili

Makes 6 servings

> 1½ pounds lean ground beef
> 1 medium onion, chopped
> 2 tablespoons chili powder
> 1 can (19 ounces) red kidney beans, rinsed and drained
> 1 jar (26 to 28 ounces) RAGÚ® Old World Style® Pasta Sauce
> 1 cup shredded Cheddar cheese (about 4 ounces)
> Hot cooked rice (optional)

1. In 12-inch skillet, brown ground beef with onion and chili powder over medium-high heat, stirring occasionally. Stir in beans and Ragú Pasta Sauce.

2. Bring to a boil over high heat. Reduce heat to low and simmer covered, stirring occasionally, 20 minutes. Top with cheese. Serve, if desired, over hot cooked rice.

Hearty Chicken and Rice Soup

Cheddar Broccoli Soup

Makes 6 (1-cup) servings

1 tablespoon BERTOLLI® Olive Oil
1 rib celery, chopped (about ½ cup)
1 carrot, chopped (about ½ cup)
1 small onion, chopped (about ½ cup)
½ teaspoon dried thyme leaves, crushed (optional)
2 cans (13¾ ounces each) chicken broth
1 jar (16 ounces) RAGÚ® Cheese Creations!® Double Cheddar Sauce
1 box (10 ounces) frozen chopped broccoli, thawed and drained

In 3-quart saucepan, heat oil over medium heat and cook celery, carrot, onion and thyme 3 minutes or until vegetables are almost tender. Add chicken broth and bring to a boil over high heat. *Reduce heat* to medium and simmer, uncovered, 10 minutes.

In food processor or blender, purée vegetable mixture until smooth; return to saucepan. Stir in Ragú Cheese Creations! Sauce and broccoli. Cook 10 minutes or until heated through.

Spicy Quick and Easy Chili

Makes 4 servings

Prep and Cook Time: 15 minutes

1 pound ground beef
1 large clove garlic, minced
1 can (15¼ ounces) DEL MONTE® Whole Kernel Golden Sweet Corn, drained
1 can (16 ounces) kidney beans, drained
1½ cups salsa, mild, medium or hot
1 can (4 ounces) diced green chiles, undrained

1. Brown meat with garlic in large saucepan; drain.

2. Add remaining ingredients. Simmer, uncovered, 10 minutes, stirring occasionally. Sprinkle with chopped green onions, if desired.

Cheddar Broccoli Soup

Italian Rustico Soup

Makes 12 servings

> **1 cup BARILLA® Elbows**
> **2 tablespoons olive or vegetable oil**
> **1 pound fresh escarole or spinach, chopped**
> **1 small onion, chopped**
> **2 teaspoons minced garlic**
> **4 cups water**
> **2 cans (14½ ounces each) chicken broth**
> **1 jar (26 ounces) BARILLA® Lasagna & Casserole Sauce or**
>   **Marinara Pasta Sauce**
> **1 can (15 ounces) white beans, drained**
> **2 teaspoons balsamic or red wine vinegar**
> **Grated Parmesan cheese (optional)**

1. Cook elbows according to package directions; drain.

2. Heat oil in 4-quart Dutch oven or large pot. Add escarole, onion and garlic; cook over medium heat, stirring occasionally, about 5 minutes or until onion is tender.

3. Stir in cooked elbows and remaining ingredients except cheese; heat to boiling. *Reduce heat;* cook, uncovered, 15 minutes, stirring occasionally. Serve with cheese, if desired.

Italian Rustico Soup

Velveeta® Spicy Southwest Corn Cheese Soup

Makes 4 (1-cup) servings

Prep Time: 15 minutes
Cook Time: 10 minutes

>   1 package (10 ounces) frozen sweet corn, thawed, drained
>   1 clove garlic, minced
>   1 tablespoon butter or margarine
>   ¾ pound (12 ounces) VELVEETA® Pasteurized Prepared Cheese Product, cut up
>   1 can (4 ounces) chopped green chilies
>   ¾ cup chicken broth
>   ¾ cup milk
>   2 tablespoons chopped fresh cilantro

1. Cook and stir corn and garlic in butter in large saucepan on medium-high heat until tender. Reduce heat to medium.

2. Stir in remaining ingredients; cook until VELVEETA is melted and soup is thoroughly heated. Top each serving with crushed tortilla chips, if desired.

Black and White Chili

Makes 6 (1-cup) servings

Prep and Cook Time: 30 minutes

>   1 pound chicken tenders, cut into ¾-inch pieces
>   1 cup coarsely chopped onion
>   1 can (15½ ounces) Great Northern beans, drained
>   1 can (15 ounces) black beans, drained
>   1 can (14½ ounces) Mexican-style stewed tomatoes, undrained
>   2 tablespoons Texas-style chili powder seasoning mix

1. Spray large saucepan with nonstick cooking spray; heat over medium heat until hot. Add chicken and onion; cook and stir over medium to medium-high heat 5 to 8 minutes or until chicken is browned.

2. Stir remaining ingredients into saucepan; bring to a boil. Reduce heat to low; simmer, uncovered, 10 minutes.

Velveeta® Spicy Southwest Corn Cheese Soup

Seafood Gumbo

Makes 4 servings

1 bag SUCCESS® Rice
1 tablespoon reduced-calorie margarine
¼ cup chopped onion
¼ cup chopped green bell pepper
2 cloves garlic, minced
1 can (28 ounces) whole tomatoes, cut up, undrained
2 cups chicken broth
½ teaspoon ground red pepper
½ teaspoon dried thyme leaves, crushed
½ teaspoon dried basil leaves, crushed
¾ pound white fish, cut into 1-inch pieces
1 package (10 ounces) frozen cut okra, thawed and drained
½ pound shrimp, peeled and deveined

Prepare rice according to package directions.

Melt margarine in large saucepan over medium-high heat. Add onion, green pepper and garlic; cook and stir until crisp-tender. Stir in tomatoes with juice, broth, red pepper, thyme and basil. Bring to a boil. *Reduce heat* to low; simmer, uncovered, until thoroughly heated, 10 to 15 minutes. Stir in fish, okra and shrimp; simmer until fish flakes easily with fork and shrimp curl and turn pink. Add rice; heat thoroughly, stirring occasionally, 5 to 8 minutes.

Seafood Gumbo

Spicy Lentil and Chick-Pea Soup

Makes 6 servings

     ½ **cup dried chick-peas (garbanzo beans)**
     4 **cans (14 ounces each) ⅓-less-salt chicken broth**
     1 **cup dried lentils**
     1 **large onion, chopped**
     1 **rib celery, chopped**
     1 **teaspoon ground turmeric**
     ½ **teaspoon salt**
     ½ **teaspoon ground cinnamon**
     ½ **teaspoon black pepper**
     ¼ **teaspoon ground ginger**
     ¼ **teaspoon ground red pepper**
     ¼ **cup uncooked rice**
     3 **cups chopped ripe tomatoes**
     ¼ **cup chopped fresh parsley**
     2 **tablespoons chopped fresh cilantro**
     6 **lemon wedges**

1. Sort and rinse chick-peas; place in large saucepan. Cover with water and let soak overnight; drain chick-peas and return to saucepan. Add chicken broth to saucepan; bring to a boil over high heat. *Reduce heat* to low; cover and simmer 1 hour.

2. Sort and rinse lentils; add to chick-peas with onion, celery, turmeric, salt, cinnamon, black pepper, ginger and ground red pepper. Cover and simmer 45 minutes or until lentils are tender.

3. Stir in rice and tomatoes; bring to a boil over medium-high heat. Reduce heat to low; cover and simmer 20 to 25 minutes or until rice is tender.

4. Stir in parsley and cilantro; simmer 5 minutes. Serve with lemon wedges; garnish with additional fresh cilantro, if desired.

Spicy Lentil and Chick-Pea Soup

home-style dinners

Italian-Style Meat Loaf

Makes 8 servings

Prep Time: 10 minutes
Cook Time: 75 minutes
Standing Time: 10 minutes

> 1 **egg**
> 1½ **pounds lean ground beef or turkey**
> 8 **ounces hot or mild Italian sausage, casings removed**
> 1 **cup CONTADINA® Seasoned Bread Crumbs**
> 1 **can (8 ounces) CONTADINA Tomato Sauce, divided**
> 1 **cup finely chopped onion**
> ½ **cup finely chopped green bell pepper**

1. Beat egg lightly in large bowl. Add beef, sausage, bread crumbs, ¾ cup tomato sauce, onion and bell pepper; mix well.

2. Press into *ungreased* 9×5-inch loaf pan. Bake, uncovered, in preheated 350°F oven for 60 minutes.

3. Spoon remaining tomato sauce over meat loaf. Bake 15 minutes longer or until no longer pink in center; drain. Let stand for 10 minutes before serving.

Italian-Style Meat Loaf

Buttermilk Ranch Fried Chicken

Makes 4 to 6 servings

**2½ to 3 pounds frying chicken pieces
WESSON® Vegetable Oil
2¼ cups all-purpose flour
1¼ tablespoons dried dill weed
1½ teaspoons salt
¾ teaspoon pepper
2½ cups buttermilk**

Rinse chicken and pat dry; set aside. Fill a large deep-fry pot or electric skillet to no more than half its depth with Wesson® Oil. Heat oil to 325°F to 350°F. In a medium bowl, combine flour, dill, salt and pepper. Fill another bowl with buttermilk. Place chicken, one piece at a time, in buttermilk; shake off excess liquid. Coat lightly in flour mixture; shake off excess flour. Dip once again in buttermilk and flour mixture. Fry chicken, a few pieces at a time, skin side down, for 10 to 14 minutes. Turn chicken and fry 12 to 15 minutes longer or until juices run clear; drain on paper towels. Let stand 7 minutes before serving.

Cook's Tip: To reduce frying time by 7 to 9 minutes per side, simply cook unbreaded chicken in boiling water for 15 minutes; remove and cool completely before proceeding with recipe.

Buttermilk Ranch Fried Chicken

Skillet Pork Chops with Maple Apples

Makes 4 servings

Prep and Cook Time: 26 minutes

- 1 package (12 ounces) uncooked egg noodles
- 1 teaspoon dried oregano leaves
- 1 teaspoon dried thyme leaves
- ½ teaspoon salt
- ½ teaspoon ground nutmeg
- ¼ teaspoon black pepper
- 4 well-trimmed center-cut pork chops, cut ½ inch thick
- 2 tablespoons margarine or butter, divided
- 1 red apple
- ¼ cup maple syrup
- 2 tablespoons lemon juice
- ½ teaspoon ground ginger

1. Prepare noodles according to package directions; drain.

2. While noodles are cooking, combine oregano, thyme, salt, nutmeg and pepper in small bowl; sprinkle over pork chops.

3. Heat 1 tablespoon margarine in large skillet until hot. Add pork chops and cook over medium heat 5 to 7 minutes per side or until pork is barely pink in center. Remove from skillet and cover to keep warm.

4. Cut apple in half; core and cut into slices. Add remaining 1 tablespoon margarine and apple to skillet. Cook, stirring occasionally, about 3 minutes or until tender. Stir in syrup, lemon juice, ginger and additional salt and pepper to taste. Cook about 2 minutes or until slightly thickened.

5. Serve pork chops and apple mixture over noodles.

Cook's Tip: For a special touch, garnish with fresh oregano leaves.

Skillet Pork Chop with Maple Apples

Spaghetti Sauce

Makes 8 servings

Prep Time: 8 minutes
Cook Time: 35 minutes

> 1 pound dry pasta
> 1 pound mild Italian sausage, casing removed
> 1 cup chopped onion
> 1 clove garlic, minced
> ½ cup sliced fresh mushrooms
> 1 can (28 ounces) CONTADINA® Recipe Ready Crushed Tomatoes
> 1 can (15 ounces) CONTADINA Tomato Sauce
> ½ teaspoon dried oregano leaves, crushed
> ¼ teaspoon dried basil leaves, crushed

1. Cook pasta according to package directions; drain and keep warm.

2. Meanwhile, brown sausage with onion and garlic in large skillet, stirring to break up sausage. Stir in mushrooms, crushed tomatoes, tomato sauce, oregano and basil.

3. Bring to a boil. Reduce heat to low; simmer, uncovered, for 30 minutes, stirring occasionally. Serve over pasta.

Spaghetti Sauce

home-style**dinners**

Roasted Turkey Breast with Cherry & Apple Rice Stuffing

Makes 6 to 8 servings

> **3¾ cups water**
> **3 boxes UNCLE BEN'S® Long Grain & Wild Rice Butter & Herb Fast Cook Recipe**
> **½ cup butter or margarine, divided**
> **½ cup dried red tart cherries**
> **1 large apple, peeled and chopped (about 1 cup)**
> **½ cup sliced almonds, toasted***
> **1 bone-in turkey breast (5 to 6 pounds)**

*To toast almonds, place them on a baking sheet. Bake 10 to 12 minutes in preheated 325°F oven or until golden brown, stirring occasionally.

1. In large saucepan, combine water, rice, contents of seasoning packets, 3 tablespoons butter and cherries. Bring to a boil. Cover; *reduce heat* to low and simmer 25 minutes or until all water is absorbed. Stir in apple and almonds; set aside.

2. Preheat oven to 325°F. Place turkey breast, skin side down, on rack in roasting pan. Loosely fill breast cavity with rice stuffing. (Place any remaining stuffing in greased baking dish; cover and refrigerate. Bake alongside turkey for 35 to 40 minutes or until heated through.)

3. Place sheet of heavy-duty foil over stuffing, molding it slightly over sides of turkey. Carefully invert turkey, skin side up, on rack. Melt remaining 5 tablespoons butter; brush some of butter over surface of turkey.

4. Roast turkey, uncovered, 1 hour; baste with melted butter. Continue roasting 1¼ to 1¾ hours, basting occasionally with melted butter, until meat thermometer inserted into center of thickest part of turkey breast, not touching bone, registers 170°F. Let turkey stand, covered, 15 minutes before carving.

Roasted Turkey Breast with Cherry & Apple Rice Stuffing

Beef and Vegetables in Rich Burgundy Sauce

Makes 6 to 8 servings

- 1 package (8 ounces) sliced mushrooms
- 1 package (8 ounces) baby carrots
- 1 medium green bell pepper, cut into thin strips
- 1 boneless beef chuck roast (about 2½ pounds)
- 1 can (10½ ounces) condensed golden mushroom soup
- ¼ cup dry red wine or beef broth
- 1 tablespoon Worcestershire sauce
- 1 package (1 ounce) dry onion soup mix
- ¼ teaspoon black pepper
- 2 tablespoons water
- 3 tablespoons cornstarch
- 4 cups hot cooked noodles
- Chopped fresh parsley (optional)

SLOW COOKER DIRECTIONS

1. Place mushrooms, carrots and bell pepper in slow cooker. Place roast on top of vegetables. Combine mushroom soup, wine, Worcestershire sauce, soup mix and black pepper in medium bowl; mix well. Pour soup mixture over roast. Cover and cook on LOW 8 to 10 hours.

2. Blend water into cornstarch in cup until smooth; set aside. Transfer roast to cutting board; cover with foil. Let stand 10 to 15 minutes before slicing.

3. Turn slow cooker to HIGH. Stir cornstarch mixture into vegetable mixture; cover and cook 10 minutes or until thickened. Serve over cooked noodles. Garnish with parsley, if desired.

Beef and Vegetables in Rich Burgundy Sauce

Chicken Pot Pie

Makes about 6 cups or 4 servings

> 1½ **pounds chicken pieces, skinned**
> 1 **cup chicken broth**
> ½ **teaspoon salt**
> ¼ **teaspoon black pepper**
> 1 to 1½ **cups 2% milk**
> 3 **tablespoons margarine or butter**
> 1 **medium onion, chopped**
> 1 **cup sliced celery**
> ⅓ **cup all-purpose flour**
> 2 **cups frozen mixed vegetables (broccoli, carrots and**
> **cauliflower combination), thawed**
> ½ **teaspoon dried thyme leaves**
> 1 **tablespoon chopped fresh parsley** *or* 1 **teaspoon dried**
> **parsley**
> 1 **(9-inch) refrigerated pastry crust**
> 1 **egg, slightly beaten**

1. Combine chicken, chicken broth, salt and pepper in large saucepan over medium-high heat. Bring to a boil. Reduce heat to low. Cover; simmer 30 minutes or until juices run clear.

2. Remove chicken and let cool. Pour remaining chicken broth mixture into glass measure. Let stand; spoon off fat. Add enough milk to broth mixture to equal 2½ cups. Remove chicken from bones and cut into ½-inch pieces.

3. Melt margarine in same saucepan over medium heat. Add onion and celery. Cook and stir 3 minutes. Stir in flour until well blended. Gradually stir in broth mixture. Cook, stirring constantly, until sauce thickens and boils. Add chicken, vegetables, thyme and parsley. Pour into 1½-quart deep casserole.

4. Preheat oven to 400°F. Roll out pastry 1 inch larger than diameter of casserole on lightly floured surface. Cut slits in pastry for venting air. Place pastry on top of casserole. Roll edges and cut away extra pastry; flute edges. Reroll scraps to cut into decorative designs. Place on top of pastry. Brush pastry with beaten egg. Bake about 30 minutes until crust is golden brown and filling is bubbling.

Cook's Tip: 2 cups diced cooked chicken, 1 can (14½ ounces) chicken broth, ¼ teaspoon salt and ¼ teaspoon black pepper can be substituted for the first 4 ingredients.

Chicken Pot Pie

home-style**dinners**

Grilled Jumbo Shrimp

Makes 6 servings

24 raw jumbo shrimp, shelled and deveined
1 cup WESSON® Canola Oil
½ cup minced fresh onion
2 teaspoons dried oregano
1 teaspoon salt
1 teaspoon crushed fresh garlic
½ teaspoon dried basil
½ teaspoon dried thyme
3 tablespoons fresh lemon juice
6 long bamboo skewers, soaked in water for 20 minutes

Rinse shrimp and pat dry; set aside. In a large bowl, whisk together Wesson® Oil and *next* 6 ingredients, ending with thyme. Reserve ⅓ cup marinade; set aside. Toss shrimp in remaining marinade; cover and refrigerate 3 hours, tossing occasionally. Stir in lemon juice; let stand at room temperature for 30 minutes. Meanwhile, preheat grill or broiler. Drain shrimp; discard marinade. Thread 4 shrimp per skewer. Grill shrimp, 4 inches over hot coals, 3 minutes per side or until pink, basting with reserved ⅓ cup marinade.

Ragú® Chili Mac

Makes 4 servings

1 tablespoon olive or vegetable oil
1 medium green bell pepper, chopped
1 pound ground beef
1 jar (26 to 28 ounces) RAGÚ® Old World Style® Pasta Sauce
2 tablespoons chili powder
8 ounces elbow macaroni, cooked and drained

1. In 12-inch nonstick skillet, heat oil over medium-high heat and cook green bell pepper, stirring occasionally, 3 minutes. Add ground beef and brown, stirring occasionally; drain.

2. Stir in Ragú Pasta Sauce and chili powder. Bring to a boil over high heat. *Reduce heat* to low and simmer, covered, 10 minutes.

3. Stir in macaroni and heat through. Serve, if desired, with sour cream and shredded Cheddar cheese.

Grilled Jumbo Shrimp

Turkey Tetrazzini with Roasted Red Peppers

Makes 6 servings

Prep and Cook Time: 20 minutes

> 6 ounces uncooked egg noodles
> 3 tablespoons butter or margarine
> ¼ cup all-purpose flour
> 1 can (about 14 ounces) chicken broth
> 1 cup whipping cream
> 2 tablespoons dry sherry
> 2 cans (6 ounces each) sliced mushrooms, drained
> 1 jar (7½ ounces) roasted red peppers, drained and
> cut into ½-inch strips
> 2 cups chopped cooked turkey
> 1 teaspoon dried Italian seasoning
> ½ cup grated Parmesan cheese

1. Cook egg noodles in large saucepan according to package directions. Drain well; return noodles to saucepan.

2. While noodles are cooking, melt butter in medium saucepan over medium heat. Add flour and whisk until smooth. Add chicken broth; bring to a boil over high heat. Remove from heat. Gradually add whipping cream and sherry; stir to combine.

3. Add mushrooms and peppers to noodles; toss to combine. Add half the chicken broth mixture to noodle mixture. Combine remaining chicken broth mixture, turkey and Italian seasoning in large bowl.

4. Spoon noodle mixture into serving dish. Make a well in center of noodles and spoon in turkey mixture. Sprinkle cheese over top.

Turkey Tetrazzini with Roasted Red Peppers

Salisbury Steaks with Mushroom-Wine Sauce

Makes 4 servings

Prep and Cook Time: 20 minutes

> 1 pound lean ground beef sirloin
> ¾ teaspoon garlic salt or seasoned salt
> ¼ teaspoon black pepper
> 2 tablespoons butter or margarine
> 1 package (8 ounces) sliced button mushrooms *or*
>   2 packages (4 ounces each) sliced exotic mushrooms
> 2 tablespoons sweet vermouth or ruby port wine
> 1 jar (12 ounces) *or* 1 can (10½ ounces) beef gravy

1. Heat large heavy nonstick skillet over medium-high heat 3 minutes or until hot.* Meanwhile, combine ground sirloin, garlic salt and pepper; mix well. Shape mixture into four ¼-inch-thick oval patties.

2. Place patties in skillet as they are formed; cook 3 minutes per side or until browned. Transfer to plate. Pour off drippings.

3. Melt butter in skillet; add mushrooms. Cook and stir 2 minutes. Add vermouth; cook 1 minute. Add gravy; mix well.

4. Return patties to skillet; simmer, uncovered, over medium heat 2 minutes for medium or until desired doneness, turning meat and stirring sauce.

If pan is not heavy, use medium heat.

Cook's Tip: For a special touch, sprinkle steaks with chopped parsley or chives.

Salisbury Steak with Mushroom-Wine Sauce

Classic Fettuccine Alfredo

Makes 4 servings

- ¾ **pound uncooked dry fettuccine**
- 6 **tablespoons unsalted butter**
- ⅔ **cup heavy or whipping cream**
- ½ **teaspoon salt**
- **Generous dash white pepper**
- **Generous dash ground nutmeg**
- 1 **cup freshly grated Parmesan cheese (about 3 ounces)**
- 2 **tablespoons chopped fresh parsley**
- **Fresh Italian parsley sprig for garnish (optional)**

1. Cook fettuccine in large pot of boiling salted water 6 to 8 minutes just until al dente; remove from heat. Drain well; return to dry pot.

2. Place butter and cream in large, heavy skillet over medium-low heat. Cook and stir until butter melts and mixture bubbles. Cook and stir 2 minutes more. Stir in salt, pepper and nutmeg. Remove from heat. Gradually stir in cheese until thoroughly blended and smooth. Return briefly to heat to completely blend cheese if necessary. (Do not let sauce bubble or cheese will become lumpy and tough.)

3. Pour sauce over fettuccine in pot. Stir and toss with 2 forks over low heat 2 to 3 minutes until sauce is thickened and fettuccine is evenly coated. Sprinkle with chopped parsley. Garnish, if desired. Serve immediately.

Classic Fettuccine Alfredo

Country Roasted Chicken Dinner

Makes about 8 servings

1 envelope LIPTON® RECIPE SECRETS® Savory Herb with Garlic Soup Mix*
2 tablespoons honey
1 tablespoon water
1 tablespoon I CAN'T BELIEVE IT'S NOT BUTTER!® Spread, melted
1 roasting chicken (5 to 6 pounds)
3 pounds all-purpose and/or sweet potatoes, cut into chunks

*Also terrific with Lipton® Recipe Secrets® Golden Herb with Lemon or Golden Onion Soup Mix.

Preheat oven to 350°F.

In small bowl, blend savory herb with garlic soup mix, honey, water and I Can't Believe It's Not Butter!® Spread.

In 18×12-inch roasting pan, arrange chicken, breast side up; brush with soup mixture. Cover loosely with aluminum foil. Roast 30 minutes; drain off drippings. Arrange potatoes around chicken and continue roasting covered, stirring potatoes occasionally, 1 hour or until meat thermometer reaches 175°F and potatoes are tender. *If chicken reaches 175°F before potatoes are tender, remove chicken to serving platter and keep warm. Continue roasting potatoes until tender.*

Note: Insert meat thermometer into thickest part of thigh between breast and thigh; make sure tip does not touch bone.

Country Roasted Chicken Dinner

Onion-Apple Glazed Pork Tenderloin

Makes 4 to 6 servings

Prep Time: 5 minutes
Cook Time: 25 minutes

1 (1½- to 2-pound) boneless pork tenderloin
Ground black pepper
2 tablespoons olive or vegetable oil, divided
1 envelope LIPTON® RECIPE SECRETS® Onion Soup Mix
½ cup apple juice
2 tablespoons firmly packed brown sugar
¾ cup water
¼ cup dry red wine or water
1 tablespoon all-purpose flour

1. Preheat oven to 425°F. In small roasting pan or baking pan, arrange pork. Season with pepper and rub with 1 tablespoon oil. Roast, uncovered, 10 minutes.

2. Meanwhile, in small bowl, combine remaining 1 tablespoon oil, soup mix, apple juice and brown sugar. Pour over pork and continue roasting 10 minutes or until desired doneness. Remove pork to serving platter; cover with aluminum foil.

3. Place roasting pan over medium-high heat and bring pan juices to a boil, scraping up any browned bits from bottom of pan. Stir in water, wine and flour; boil, stirring constantly, 1 minute or until thickened.

4. To serve, thinly slice pork and serve with gravy.

Onion-Apple Glazed Pork Tenderloin

Velveeta® Tuna & Noodles

Makes 4 to 6 servings

Prep Time: 10 minutes
Cook Time: 15 minutes

> 2¼ **cups water**
> 3 **cups (6 ounces) medium egg noodles, uncooked**
> ¾ **pound (12 ounces) VELVEETA® Pasteurized Prepared Cheese Product, cut up**
> 1 **package (16 ounces) frozen vegetable blend, thawed, drained**
> 1 **can (6 ounces) tuna, drained, flaked**
> ¼ **teaspoon black pepper**

1. Bring water to boil in saucepan. Stir in noodles. Reduce heat to medium-low; cover. Simmer 8 minutes or until noodles are tender.

2. Add VELVEETA, vegetables, tuna and pepper; stir until VELVEETA is melted.

Stuffed Green Peppers

Makes 6 servings

> 6 **medium to large green bell peppers**
> 1 **pound BOB EVANS® Original Recipe Roll Sausage**
> 2 **cups tomato sauce**
> 2 **cups water**
> 1 **small onion, chopped**
> 1 **cup uncooked rice**
> **Sliced green onion (optional)**

Preheat oven to 350°F. Slice off tops from peppers; scrape out centers to remove seeds and membranes. Combine all remaining ingredients except green onion in medium bowl; mix well. Evenly stuff peppers with sausage mixture. Place in lightly greased deep 3-quart casserole dish. Bake, covered, 20 minutes. Uncover; bake 5 to 10 minutes more or until peppers are fork-tender and filling is set. Garnish with green onion, if desired. Serve hot. Refrigerate leftovers.

Velveeta® Tuna & Noodles

Lasagna Supreme

Makes 8 to 10 servings

    8 ounces uncooked lasagna noodles
½ pound ground beef
½ pound mild Italian sausage, casings removed
    1 medium onion, chopped
    2 cloves garlic, minced
    1 can (14½ ounces) whole peeled tomatoes, undrained and chopped
    1 can (6 ounces) tomato paste
    2 teaspoons dried basil leaves
    1 teaspoon dried marjoram leaves
    1 can (4 ounces) sliced mushrooms, drained
    2 eggs
    2 cups (16 ounces) cream-style cottage cheese
¾ cup grated Parmesan cheese, divided
    2 tablespoons dried parsley flakes
½ teaspoon salt
½ teaspoon black pepper
    2 cups (8 ounces) shredded Cheddar cheese
    3 cups (12 ounces) shredded mozzarella cheese

1. Cook lasagna noodles according to package directions; drain.

2. Cook meats, onion and garlic in large skillet over medium-high heat until meat is brown, stirring to separate meat. Drain drippings from skillet.

3. Add tomatoes with juice, tomato paste, basil and marjoram. Reduce heat to low. Cover; simmer 15 minutes, stirring often. Stir in mushrooms; set aside.

4. Preheat oven to 375°F. Beat eggs in large bowl; add cottage cheese, ½ cup Parmesan cheese, parsley, salt and pepper. Mix well.

5. Place half the noodles in bottom of greased 13×9-inch baking pan. Spread half the cottage cheese mixture over noodles, then half the meat mixture and half the Cheddar cheese and mozzarella cheese. Repeat layers. Sprinkle with remaining ¼ cup Parmesan cheese.

6. Bake lasagna 40 to 45 minutes or until bubbly. Let stand 10 minutes before cutting.

Cook's Tip: Lasagna may be assembled, covered and refrigerated up to 2 days in advance. Bake, uncovered, in preheated 375°F oven 60 minutes or until bubbly.

Lasagna Supreme

comforting sides

Potatoes au Gratin

Makes 6 to 8 servings

    4 to 6 medium unpeeled baking potatoes (about 2 pounds)
    2 cups (8 ounces) shredded Cheddar cheese
    1 cup (4 ounces) shredded Swiss cheese
    2 tablespoons butter or margarine
    3 tablespoons all-purpose flour
2½ cups milk
    2 tablespoons Dijon mustard
    ¼ teaspoon salt
    ¼ teaspoon black pepper

1. Preheat oven to 400°F. Grease 13×9-inch baking dish.

2. Cut potatoes into thin slices. Layer potatoes in prepared dish. Top with cheeses.

3. Melt butter in medium saucepan over medium heat. Stir in flour; cook 1 minute. Stir in milk, mustard, salt and pepper; bring to a boil. Reduce heat and cook, stirring constantly, until mixture thickens. Pour milk mixture over cheese. Cover pan with foil.

4. Bake 30 minutes. Remove foil and bake 15 to 20 minutes more until potatoes are tender and top is brown. Remove from oven and let stand 10 minutes before serving.

Potatoes au Gratin

Double-Baked Potatoes

Makes 6 servings

3 large baking potatoes
4 tablespoons fat-free (skim) milk, warmed
1 cup (4 ounces) shredded reduced-fat Cheddar cheese
¾ cup corn
½ teaspoon chili powder
1 tablespoon finely chopped fresh oregano *or* ½ teaspoon dried oregano leaves
1 cup chopped onion
½ to 1 cup chopped poblano chili peppers or green bell pepper
3 cloves garlic, minced
½ teaspoon salt
¼ teaspoon black pepper
3 tablespoons chopped fresh parsley or cilantro

1. Preheat oven to 400°F. Scrub potatoes under running water with soft vegetable brush; rinse. Pierce each potato with fork. Wrap each potato in foil. Bake about 1 hour or until fork-tender. Remove potatoes; cool slightly. *Reduce oven temperature to 350°F.*

2. Cut potatoes in half lengthwise; scoop out inside being careful not to tear shells. Set shells aside. Beat potatoes in large bowl with electric mixer until coarsely mashed. Add milk; beat until smooth. Stir in cheese, corn, chili powder and oregano. Set aside.

3. Spray medium skillet with nonstick cooking spray. Add onion, poblano peppers and garlic; cook and stir 5 to 8 minutes or until tender. Stir in salt and pepper.

4. Spoon potato mixture into reserved potato shells. Sprinkle with onion mixture. Place stuffed potatoes in small baking pan. Bake 20 to 30 minutes or until heated through. Sprinkle with parsley.

Double-Baked Potato

Velveeta® Ultimate Macaroni & Cheese

Makes 4 to 6 servings

Prep Time: 5 minutes
Cook Time: 15 minutes

> 2 cups (8 ounces) elbow macaroni, uncooked
> 1 pound (16 ounces) VELVEETA® Pasteurized Prepared Cheese Product, cut up
> ½ cup milk
> Dash pepper

1. Cook macaroni as directed on package; drain well. Return to same pan.

2. Add VELVEETA, milk and pepper to same pan. Stir on low heat until VELVEETA is melted. Serve immediately.

Bow Tie Pasta Salad

Makes about 8 side-dish servings

Prep Time: 5 minutes
Cook Time: 20 minutes

> 1 package (16 ounces) uncooked bow ties, rotini, ziti or other shaped pasta
> 1 bag (16 ounces) BIRDS EYE® frozen Farm Fresh Mixtures Broccoli, Cauliflower and Carrots*
> 1 cup Italian, creamy Italian or favorite salad dressing
> 1 bunch green onions, thinly sliced
> 1 cup pitted ripe olives, halved (optional)

Or, substitute any other Birds Eye® frozen Farm Fresh Mixtures variety.

• Cook pasta according to package directions; drain.

• Cook vegetables according to package directions; drain.

• Combine pasta and vegetables with remaining ingredients in large bowl. Cover and chill until ready to serve.

Velveeta® Ultimate Macaroni & Cheese

comfortingsides

Broccoli Casserole with Crumb Topping

Makes 6 servings

> 2 slices day-old white bread, coarsely crumbled (about 1¼ cups)
> ½ cup shredded mozzarella cheese (about 2 ounces)
> 2 tablespoons chopped fresh parsley (optional)
> 2 tablespoons olive or vegetable oil, divided
> 1 clove garlic, finely chopped
> 6 cups broccoli florets and/or cauliflowerets
> 1 envelope LIPTON® RECIPE SECRETS® Onion Soup Mix
> 1 cup water
> 1 large tomato, chopped

1. In small bowl, combine bread crumbs, cheese, parsley, 1 tablespoon oil and garlic; set aside.

2. In 12-inch skillet, heat remaining 1 tablespoon oil over medium heat and cook broccoli, stirring frequently, 2 minutes.

3. Stir in onion soup mix blended with water. Bring to a boil over high heat. Reduce heat to low and simmer, uncovered, stirring occasionally, 8 minutes or until broccoli is almost tender. Add tomato and simmer 2 minutes.

4. Spoon vegetable mixture into 1½-quart casserole; top with bread crumb mixture. Broil 1½ minutes or until crumbs are golden and cheese is melted.

Creamed Spinach Casserole

Makes 6 to 8 servings

> 2 packages (10 ounces each) frozen chopped spinach, thawed, well drained
> 2 packages (8 ounces each) PHILADELPHIA® Cream Cheese, softened
> 1 teaspoon lemon and pepper seasoning salt
> ⅓ cup crushed seasoned croutons

MIX spinach, cream cheese and seasoning salt until well blended.

SPOON into 1-quart casserole. Sprinkle with crushed croutons.

BAKE at 350°F for 25 to 30 minutes or until thoroughly heated.

Broccoli Casserole with Crumb Topping

Country-Style Mashed Potatoes

Makes 8 (¾-cup) servings

> 4 pounds baking potatoes, unpeeled and cut into 1-inch pieces
> 6 large cloves garlic, peeled
> ½ cup nonfat sour cream
> ½ cup fat-free (skim) milk, warmed
> 2 tablespoons margarine
> 2 tablespoons finely chopped fresh rosemary *or* 1 teaspoon dried rosemary
> 2 tablespoons finely chopped fresh thyme *or* ½ teaspoon dried thyme leaves
> 2 tablespoons finely chopped fresh parsley *or* 1 teaspoon dried parsley flakes

1. Place potatoes and garlic in medium saucepan; cover with water. Bring to a boil. Reduce heat and simmer, covered, about 15 minutes or until potatoes are fork-tender. Drain well.

2. Place potatoes and garlic in large bowl. Beat with electric mixer just until mashed. Beat in sour cream, milk and margarine until almost smooth. Mix in rosemary, thyme and parsley.

Honey-Glazed Carrots

Makes 6 servings

> 3 cups sliced carrots
> 6 tablespooons honey
> 2 tablespoons butter or margarine
> 2 tablespoons chopped fresh parsley
> 1½ teaspoons Dijon mustard (optional)

1. Bring 2 inches of salted water to a boil in medium saucepan over high heat. Add carrots and return to a boil. Reduce heat to medium. Cover and cook 8 to 12 minutes or until carrots are crisp-tender.

2. Drain carrots; return to saucepan. Stir in honey, butter, parsley and mustard, if desired. Cook and stir over low heat until carrots are glazed.

Country-Style Mashed Potatoes

comfortingsides

Green Beans with Toasted Pecans

Makes 4 servings

> 3 tablespoons I CAN'T BELIEVE IT'S NOT BUTTER!® Spread, melted
> 1 teaspoon sugar
> ¼ teaspoon garlic powder
> Pinch ground red pepper
> Salt to taste
> ⅓ cup chopped pecans
> 1 pound green beans

In small bowl, blend I Can't Believe It's Not Butter! Spread, sugar, garlic powder, pepper and salt.

In 12-inch nonstick skillet, heat 2 teaspoons garlic mixture over medium-high heat and cook pecans, stirring frequently, 2 minutes or until pecans are golden. Remove pecans and set aside.

In same skillet, heat remaining garlic mixture and stir in green beans. Cook, covered, over medium heat, stirring occasionally, 6 minutes or until green beans are tender. Stir in pecans.

Carrot Raisin Salad with Citrus Dressing

Makes 8 servings

> ¾ cup reduced-fat sour cream
> ¼ cup nonfat milk
> 1 tablespoon honey
> 1 tablespoon orange juice concentrate
> 1 tablespoon lime juice
> Peel of 1 medium orange, grated
> ¼ teaspoon salt
> 8 medium carrots, peeled and coarsely shredded (about 2 cups)
> ¼ cup raisins
> ⅓ cup chopped cashews

Combine sour cream, milk, honey, orange juice concentrate, lime juice, orange peel and salt in small bowl. Blend well and set aside.

Combine carrots and raisins in bowl. Pour dressing over; toss to coat. Cover; refrigerate 30 minutes. Toss before serving. Top with cashews.

Green Beans with Toasted Pecans

Confetti Scalloped Corn

Makes 6 servings

1 egg, beaten
1 cup skim milk
1 cup coarsely crushed saltine crackers (about 22 two-inch square crackers), divided
¼ teaspoon salt
⅛ teaspoon pepper
1 can (16½ ounces) cream-style corn
¼ cup finely chopped onion
1 jar (2 ounces) chopped pimiento, drained
1 tablespoon CRISCO® Oil*
1 tablespoon chopped fresh parsley

Use your favorite Crisco Oil product.

1. Heat oven to 350°F.

2. Combine egg, milk, ⅔ cup cracker crumbs, salt and pepper in medium bowl. Stir in corn, onion and pimiento. Pour into *ungreased* one-quart casserole.

3. Combine remaining ⅓ cup cracker crumbs with oil in small bowl. Toss to coat. Sprinkle over corn mixture.

4. Bake at 350°F for one hour or until knife inserted into center comes out clean. *Do not overbake.* Sprinkle with parsley. Let stand 5 to 10 minutes before serving. Garnish, if desired.

Salsa Macaroni & Cheese

Makes 4 servings

Prep Time: 5 minutes
Cook Time: 15 minutes

1 jar (16 ounces) RAGÚ® Cheese Creations!® Double Cheddar Sauce
1 cup prepared mild salsa
8 ounces elbow macaroni, cooked and drained

1. In 2-quart saucepan, heat Ragú Cheese Creations! Sauce over medium heat. Stir in salsa; heat through.

2. Toss with hot macaroni. Serve immediately.

Confetti Scalloped Corn

Layered Orange Pineapple Mold

Makes 10 servings

Preparation Time: 20 minutes
Refrigerating Time: 6 hours

> 1 can (20 ounces) crushed pineapple in juice, undrained
> Cold water
> 1½ cups boiling water
> 1 package (8-serving size) or 2 packages (4-serving size) JELL-O® Brand Orange Flavor Gelatin Dessert
> 1 package (8 ounces) PHILADELPHIA® Cream Cheese, softened

DRAIN pineapple, reserving juice. Add cold water to juice to make 1½ cups.

STIR boiling water into gelatin in large bowl at least 2 minutes until completely dissolved. Stir in measured pineapple juice and water. Reserve 1 cup gelatin at room temperature.

STIR ½ of the crushed pineapple into remaining gelatin. Pour into 6-cup mold. Refrigerate about 2 hours or until set but not firm (gelatin should stick to finger when touched and should mound).

STIR reserved 1 cup gelatin gradually into cream cheese in medium bowl with wire whisk until smooth. Stir in remaining crushed pineapple. Pour over gelatin layer in mold.

REFRIGERATE 4 hours or until firm. Unmold. Garnish as desired.

Easy Pineapple Slaw

Makes 4 to 6 servings

Prep Time: 5 minutes

> 1 can (15¼ ounces) DEL MONTE® Pineapple Tidbits In Its Own Juice
> ⅓ cup mayonnaise
> 2 tablespoons vinegar
> 6 cups coleslaw mix or shredded cabbage

1. Drain pineapple, reserving 3 tablespoons juice.

2. Combine reserved juice, mayonnaise and vinegar; toss with pineapple and coleslaw mix. Season to taste.

Layered Orange Pineapple Mold

best-loved desserts

Chocolate Chip Pecan Pie

Makes 1 (9-inch) pie

CRUST

> **1 unbaked 9-inch Classic CRISCO® Single Crust (recipe page 78)**

FILLING

> **4 eggs**
> **1 cup sugar**
> **1 cup light corn syrup**
> **3 tablespoons butter or margarine, melted**
> **1 teaspoon vanilla**
> **¼ teaspoon salt**
> **2 cups pecan halves**
> **½ cup semi-sweet chocolate chips**
> **1 tablespoon plus 1½ teaspoons bourbon (optional)**

1. Heat oven to 375°F. Place cooling rack on counter for cooling pie.

2. For filling, beat eggs in large bowl at low speed of electric mixer until blended. Stir in sugar, corn syrup, butter, vanilla and salt with spoon until blended. Stir in nuts, chocolate chips and bourbon. Pour into unbaked pie crust.

3. Bake at 375°F for 55 to 60 minutes or until set. *Do not overbake.* Cover edge of pie with foil, if necessary, to prevent overbrowning. Remove pie to cooling rack to cool completely. Cool to room temperature before serving. Refrigerate leftover pie.

Chocolate Chip Pecan Pie

Lemon Dream Pie

Makes 8 servings

    1 prepared or homemade 9-inch pie shell
1½ cups water
  1 cup honey
  ½ cup lemon juice
  ⅓ cup cornstarch
  2 tablespoons butter or margarine
  1 teaspoon grated lemon peel
  ¼ teaspoon salt
  4 egg yolks, lightly beaten
1½ cups heavy whipping cream, whipped to soft peaks

Bake empty pie shell according to package directions until golden brown. In medium saucepan, combine water, honey, lemon juice, cornstarch, butter, lemon peel and salt. Bring to a boil, stirring constantly. Boil for 5 minutes. Remove from heat. Stir small amount into yolks. Pour yolk mixture back into honey mixture; mix thoroughly. Pour into pie shell. Chill. To serve, top with whipped cream.

Favorite recipe from *National Honey Board*

Classic Crisco® Single Crust

Makes 8- to 9-inch single crust

1⅓ cups all-purpose flour
 ½ teaspoon salt
 ½ CRISCO® Stick or ½ cup CRISCO® Shortening
 3 tablespoons cold water

1. Spoon flour into measuring cup and level. Combine flour and salt in medium bowl. Cut in shortening using pastry blender or 2 knives until all flour is blended to form pea-size chunks.

2. Sprinkle with water, 1 tablespoon at a time. Toss lightly with fork until dough forms a ball.

3. Press dough between hands to form 5- to 6-inch "pancake." Flour rolling surface and rolling pin lightly. Roll dough into circle. Trim 1 inch larger than upside-down pie plate. Loosen dough carefully.

4. Fold dough into quarters. Unfold and press into pie plate. Fold edge under. Flute.

Lemon Dream Pie

Southern Banana Pudding

Makes 8 servings

Preparation Time: 30 minutes
Baking Time: 15 minutes

> 1 package (4-serving size) JELL-O® Vanilla or Banana Cream
>   Flavor Cook & Serve Pudding & Pie Filling *(not Instant)*
> 2½ cups milk
> 2 egg yolks, well beaten
> 30 to 35 vanilla wafers
> 2 large bananas, sliced
> 2 egg whites
>   Dash salt
> ¼ cup sugar

HEAT oven to 350°F.

STIR pudding mix into milk in medium saucepan. Add egg yolks. Stirring constantly, cook on medium heat until mixture comes to full boil. Remove from heat.

ARRANGE layer of cookies on bottom and up side of 1½-quart baking dish. Add layer of banana slices; top with ⅓ of the pudding. Repeat layers twice, ending with pudding.

BEAT egg whites and salt in medium bowl with electric mixer on high speed until foamy. Gradually add sugar, beating until stiff peaks form. Spoon meringue mixture lightly onto pudding, spreading to edge of dish to seal.

BAKE 10 to 15 minutes or until meringue is lightly browned. Serve warm or refrigerate until ready to serve.

Southern Banana Pudding

Brandied Peach Cobbler

Makes 6 servings

FILLING

- **6 cups fresh sliced peaches (3 pounds)** *or* **2 (16-ounce) packages frozen sliced peaches**
- **½ cup sugar**
- **¼ cup brandy**
- **1 tablespoon corn starch**
- **1 tablespoon fresh lemon juice**
- **1 teaspoon brandy extract**
- **½ teaspoon cinnamon**
- **PAM® No-Stick Cooking Spray**

TOPPING

- **1 cup all-purpose flour**
- **⅔ cup sugar**
- **1 tablespoon baking powder**
- **1 teaspoon cinnamon**
- **½ teaspoon salt**
- **½ cup WESSON® Vegetable Oil**
- **¼ cup milk**
- **½ cup chopped pecans**
- **Homemade vanilla ice cream**

For filling, in a large bowl, combine *all* filling ingredients *except* PAM® Cooking Spray. Let stand 30 minutes, stirring often. Meanwhile, preheat oven to 375°F and spray an 11×7×2-inch baking dish with Pam® Cooking Spray.

For topping, in medium bowl, combine flour, sugar, baking powder, cinnamon and salt; mix well. Add Wesson® Oil and milk; blend well. Fold in pecans. Pour peach mixture into baking dish. Evenly drop topping mixture by rounded tablespoons over peach mixture. Bake 45 to 55 minutes or until brown and bubbly. Serve cold or at room temperature with homemade vanilla ice cream.

Brandied Peach Cobbler

Butter Toffee Chocolate Chip Crunch

Makes about 4 dozen cookies

   1 cup firmly packed light brown sugar
   ¾ Butter Flavor **CRISCO**® Stick or ¾ cup Butter Flavor
      CRISCO® all-vegetable shortening plus additional for
      greasing
   1 egg
   2 tablespoons sweetened condensed milk (not evaporated
      milk)
   1 teaspoon salt
   ¾ teaspoon baking soda
   1 teaspoon vanilla
1¾ cups all-purpose flour
   ¾ cup coarsely chopped pecans
   ½ cup milk chocolate chips
   ½ cup semi-sweet chocolate chips
   2 to 4 bars (1.4 ounces each) toffee bars, finely crushed

1. Heat oven to 350°F. Grease baking sheet with shortening. Place sheets of foil on countertop for cooling cookies.

2. Combine brown sugar, shortening, egg, sweetened condensed milk, salt, baking soda and vanilla in large bowl. Beat at medium speed of electric mixer until well blended. Add flour gradually at low speed. Beat until well blended. Stir in nuts, milk chocolate chips, semi-sweet chocolate chips and crushed toffee bars with spoon. Drop by level measuring tablespoonfuls 2 inches apart onto prepared baking sheets.

3. Bake at 350°F for 10 to 12 minutes or until light golden brown. *Do not overbake.* Cool 2 minutes on baking sheet. Remove cookies to foil to cool completely.

Butter Toffee Chocolate Chip Crunch

Texas Chocolate Peanut Butter Pie

Makes one (10-inch pie)

CRUST
> 1½ cups graham cracker crumbs
> ½ cup sugar
> ½ cup (1 stick) butter, melted

FILLING
> 2 packages (8 ounces each) cream cheese, at room temperature
> 2 cups creamy peanut butter
> 1¾ cups sugar
> 1 cup heavy whipping cream

TOPPING
> ⅔ cup heavy whipping cream
> ⅓ cup sugar
> 3 ounces semisweet chocolate
> ½ cup (1 stick) butter
> 1 teaspoon vanilla extract

For crust, preheat oven to 350°F. Combine graham cracker crumbs with sugar and melted butter in medium mixing bowl. Stir until thoroughly blended. Press mixture into bottom and up side of 10-inch pie plate. Bake crust for 10 minutes; set aside to cool.

For filling, mix cream cheese, peanut butter and sugar in medium bowl until blended. Whip cream until stiff, then fold into cream cheese mixture. Spoon filling into cooled crust.

For topping, combine cream and sugar in saucepan and bring to a boil. Reduce heat and simmer for 7 minutes. Remove pan from heat. Add chocolate and butter; stir until melted. Stir in vanilla. Cool until slightly thickened. Pour evenly over pie. Refrigerate 4 to 5 hours before serving. Garnish with toasted peanuts.

Favorite recipe from *Texas Peanut Producers Board*

Texas Chocolate Peanut Butter Pie

Classic New York Cheesecake

Makes 12 servings

Prep: 15 minutes plus refrigerating
Bake: 1 hour 10 minutes

CRUST
> 1 cup HONEY MAID® Graham Cracker Crumbs
> 3 tablespoons sugar
> 3 tablespoons butter *or* margarine, melted

FILLING
> 4 packages (8 ounces each) PHILADELPHIA® Cream Cheese,
>   softened
> 1 cup sugar
> 3 tablespoons flour
> 1 tablespoon vanilla
> 1 cup BREAKSTONE'S® *or* KNUDSEN® Sour Cream
> 4 eggs

CRUST

MIX crumbs, 3 tablespoons sugar and butter; press onto bottom of 9-inch springform pan. Bake at 325°F for 10 minutes if using a silver springform pan. (Bake at 300°F for 10 minutes if using a dark nonstick springform pan.)

FILLING

BEAT cream cheese, 1 cup sugar, flour and vanilla with electric mixer on medium speed until well blended. Blend in sour cream. Add eggs, 1 at a time, mixing on low speed after each addition just until blended. Pour over crust.

BAKE at 325°F for 1 hour to 1 hour 5 minutes or until center is almost set if using a silver springform pan. (Bake at 300°F for 1 hour to 1 hour 5 minutes or until center is almost set if using a dark nonstick springform pan.) Run knife or metal spatula around rim of pan to loosen cake; cool before removing rim of pan. Refrigerate 4 hours or overnight.

Classic New York Cheesecake

Bittersweet Pecan Brownies with Caramel Sauce

Makes 8 servings

BROWNIE
- ¾ **cup all-purpose flour**
- ¼ **teaspoon baking soda**
- 4 **squares (1 ounce each) bittersweet or unsweetened chocolate, coarsely chopped**
- ½ **cup (1 stick) plus 2 tablespoons I CAN'T BELIEVE IT'S NOT BUTTER!® Spread**
- ¾ **cup sugar**
- 2 **eggs**
- ½ **cup chopped pecans**

CARAMEL SAUCE
- ¾ **cup firmly packed light brown sugar**
- 6 **tablespoons I CAN'T BELIEVE IT'S NOT BUTTER!® Spread**
- ⅓ **cup whipping or heavy cream**
- ½ **teaspoon apple cider vinegar or fresh lemon juice**

For brownie, preheat oven to 325°F. Line 8-inch square baking pan with aluminum foil, then grease and flour foil; set aside.

In small bowl, combine flour and baking soda; set aside.

In medium microwave-safe bowl, microwave chocolate and I Can't Believe It's Not Butter! Spread at HIGH (100% Power) 1 minute or until chocolate is melted; stir until smooth. With wooden spoon, beat in sugar, then eggs. Beat in flour mixture. Evenly spread into prepared pan; sprinkle with pecans.

Bake 30 minutes or until toothpick inserted into center comes out clean. On wire rack, cool completely. To remove brownies, lift edges of foil. Cut brownies into 4 squares, then cut each square into 2 triangles.

For caramel sauce, in medium saucepan, bring brown sugar, I Can't Believe It's Not Butter! Spread and cream just to a boil over high heat, stirring frequently. Cook 3 minutes. Stir in vinegar. To serve, pour caramel sauce around brownie and top, if desired, with vanilla or caramel ice cream.

Bittersweet Pecan Brownies with Caramel Sauce

acknowledgements

*The publisher would like to thank
the companies and organizations listed below
for the use of their recipes and photographs
in this publication.*

Barilla America, Inc.

Birds Eye®

Bob Evans®

CHIPS AHOY!® Chocolate Chip Cookies

ConAgra Foods®

Del Monte Corporation

Kraft Foods Holdings

National Honey Board

Riviana Foods Inc.

The J.M. Smucker Company

Texas Peanut Producers Board

Uncle Ben's Inc.

Unilever Bestfoods North America

USA Rice Federation

index

METRIC CONVERSION CHART

VOLUME MEASUREMENTS (dry)

1/8 teaspoon = 0.5 mL
1/4 teaspoon = 1 mL
1/2 teaspoon = 2 mL
3/4 teaspoon = 4 mL
1 teaspoon = 5 mL
1 tablespoon = 15 mL
2 tablespoons = 30 mL
1/4 cup = 60 mL
1/3 cup = 75 mL
1/2 cup = 125 mL
2/3 cup = 150 mL
3/4 cup = 175 mL
1 cup = 250 mL
2 cups = 1 pint = 500 mL
3 cups = 750 mL
4 cups = 1 quart = 1 L

VOLUME MEASUREMENTS (fluid)

1 fluid ounce (2 tablespoons) = 30 mL
4 fluid ounces (1/2 cup) = 125 mL
8 fluid ounces (1 cup) = 250 mL
12 fluid ounces (1 1/2 cups) = 375 mL
16 fluid ounces (2 cups) = 500 mL

WEIGHTS (mass)

1/2 ounce = 15 g
1 ounce = 30 g
3 ounces = 90 g
4 ounces = 120 g
8 ounces = 225 g
10 ounces = 285 g
12 ounces = 360 g
16 ounces = 1 pound = 450 g

DIMENSIONS

1/16 inch = 2 mm
1/8 inch = 3 mm
1/4 inch = 6 mm
1/2 inch = 1.5 cm
3/4 inch = 2 cm
1 inch = 2.5 cm

OVEN TEMPERATURES

250°F = 120°C
275°F = 140°C
300°F = 150°C
325°F = 160°C
350°F = 180°C
375°F = 190°C
400°F = 200°C
425°F = 220°C
450°F = 230°C

BAKING PAN SIZES

Utensil	Size in Inches/Quarts	Metric Volume	Size in Centimeters
Baking or Cake Pan (square or rectangular)	8×8×2	2 L	20×20×5
	9×9×2	2.5 L	23×23×5
	12×8×2	3 L	30×20×5
	13×9×2	3.5 L	33×23×5
Loaf Pan	8×4×3	1.5 L	20×10×7
	9×5×3	2 L	23×13×7
Round Layer Cake Pan	8×1½	1.2 L	20×4
	9×1½	1.5 L	23×4
Pie Plate	8×1¼	750 mL	20×3
	9×1¼	1 L	23×3
Baking Dish or Casserole	1 quart	1 L	—
	1½ quart	1.5 L	—
	2 quart	2 L	—